Erythra Thalassa

BRAIN DISRUPTED

Annette Libeskind Berkovits

Tenth Planet Press
400 East 56th Street
Apt. 16F
New York, NY 10022

Copyright @ 2020 Annette Libeskind Berkovits
annetteberkovits.com

First Edition
Paperback ISBN: 978-0998757827
E-Book ISBN: 978-0998757834
Library of Congress Control Number: 2020917126

Erythra Thalassa—When I first came across this exotic name for an ancient sea, I did not associate it with the algae that give it color. My eye zoomed to the word erythra and immediately I thought erythrocyte, a red blood cell laden with hemoglobin that gives it the crimson hue. It was then the body of water turned to a sea of blood, a terrifying image. Never did I think it would become the signal image changing our lives forever.

Besides its evocation of a hemorrhage, The Red Sea is associated with the ancient account of Israelites crossing The Red Sea. Insofar as the biblical passage connotes an insurmountable obstacle to gaining freedom, or in this case, survival, albeit altered, I find the title especially fitting for this collection.

I dedicate this book to two remarkable men

our son, Jeremy Berkovits, whose indomitable spirit, courage and optimism have helped those who love him get through the darkest days

and

to Dr. David Langer, his neurosurgeon, who is not only an extraordinary physician, but an exceptional human being who values his patients as if they were his own family.

Dr. Langer is a rare and shining example of a humanist approach to medicine. His emphasis on collaboration with peers produces outcomes that are otherwise impossible

also

to Diana Jenacaro, who has faced extraordinary adversity with courage and channeled all her energy to make it possible for Jeremy to remain at home surrounded by the love of his family. She has done so with grace and uncommon dedication while working full time and raising their two young daughters.

"Everyone can master grief, but he that has it."

William Shakespeare

Contents

Foreword

Annette Libeskind Berkovits' collection of poems, *Erythra Thalassa*, is a headlong and complete dive into the buoyancy, blood, and parting of grief. It is a book about motherhood, mothering, and the motherland of the heart.

Here is a poet facing the stroke of her son. Here is a woman holding herself up against the possibility of her son's death, his recovery, and then life, post-stroke. This is a collection about the body and the blood and the way we have no idea what mystery lives inside both. It is a book about how to cope when the body and the blood betray, surprise, fail, and ultimately, reinvigorate.

These poems investigate the parting of the waters of the red sea of life, *Erythra Thalassa*. We watch the protagonist of these situations, meditations, prayers, walk through all of it—the blood, the bone, the tendon, the heart—and then find some miraculous spirit, unimagined, on the other side. It is a parting of waters and ways; it is a book that concerns itself with the, "Dancing specks of light /one moment here, then there /then here again"—that ephemeral spirit, which lives as God, body, heartbreak, and healing.

Erythra Thalassa is a collection of poems that is not afraid to confront the break in the body and to head straight into the red.

Matthew Lippman

editor; author of six poetry collections, winner of numerous poetry book prizes: The Burnside Review; Sarabande Books; Levis Prize; The Georgetown Review Magazine Prize; The Anna Davidson Rosenberg Poetry Prize and The Jerome J. Shestack Poetry Prize from The American Poetry Review

Introduction

Any stroke is a tragedy. Strokes, sudden bolts of lightning, can strike seemingly well people of all ages. The results can range from mild for the lucky ones, to the devastating, like the massive brain bleed that changed our son's life forever. And not just his, but all his loved ones.

Courage in the face of such an event is easy to recommend, but mustering it is a heroic feat that takes every shred of psychic, emotional and physical power—every single minute, every single day. One must possess not only optimism that the future will be better, but a faith in science, God, or both. One must consciously decide to be a survivor.

In the darkest days, when my son's life teetered in the balance for weeks, then months, I was a roiling cauldron of emotions; writing helped. Somehow, pouring out my heart made the burden more manageable.

I kept writing through my son's ordeal. Eventually, the collection of poems found its own arc. I hope it tells a story of a mother's emotional struggle, the son's courage and his small physical achievements. To a healthy person "graduating" from nothing by mouth to a few tiny ice chips is, indeed, nothing, but in an epic fight to live, such tokens of progress feel like towering feats.

If this little volume eases the stress—even a tiny bit—of watching a loved one on the brink, then the sea of blood and tears will not have been entirely in vain.

Annette Libeskind Berkovits

Prima Aprilis

What's a mother to think
of her prankster baby
born just as winter snows melt
on a bright April 1st?

Was it a cruel trick to
have him, to love him,
to *kvell* at his tiny toes,
his pudgy dimpled hands?

For the mother will take
his perfection for granted.
Of course! He is her son.
He will always be flawless.

An athletic body, keen smarts,
a loving heart that takes an
old lady's hand to cross the street
feeds a beggar, fights for what's right.

But *Prima Aprilis* can bring a
surprise some 46 years later;
spring festivities long fallen silent,
a dark November day unveils
the most vicious hoax of all.

Birthday Balloons

He had the distinction of being
a show baby at the Jewish Memorial
Hospital. A hefty 10 lbs. 6 oz. baby
filled out, with a pink rosebud mouth
bundled into a taco by a *gemutlich*
German nurse. That's how it's done.

The other new mothers cooed, smiled,
admired. At the demo he was quiet,
his columbine blue eyes hinted at spring.
I stood by proudly, "I made him!" was
all I could think. I didn't know
life would bite him, rupture his vessels,
spill blood, take a chunk of his skull.

I am every mother. I know I can protect
my flesh and blood. I know I'll fight
like a warrior for whatever will make
his life better, happier, healthier.
But I am deluded. There comes a time
our powers deflate like birthday balloons.

With Apologies to the Prophet Jeremiah

How has a man once so popular remained so alone?
He has become like a hermit!
He that was great among peers, a prince among men,
has become but an infant.

He weeps, yea, he weeps on the inside, his tears invisible;
he has few comforters among those who once loved him;
some have betrayed him, many have become indifferent.

My son is in exile because of his affliction and great pain;
settled in his sick room he finds no rest, no relief;
all his friends and pursuers scattered to the four winds.

The roads to East End are mournful because
no one comes at the appointed season.
The hallway to 3B is desolate; his wife and parents grieve
while he himself suffers bitterly.

His business rivals have become the heads,
his enemies at ease. Has the Lord afflicted him
because of any sins? Why had his young daughters
been consigned to watch their father suffer?

And gone is his former splendor; his ability to nurture
living creatures gone;
His dogs that brought him joy gone;
his plants dried, wilted, dead.

He still recalls all the days of his youth;
his miseries and his joys, all his precious experiences
from days of old; when he was the king
of ultimate frisbee, the lord of the pool.

Had he sinned grievously when he wandered the world?
No. He was honored and loved by peers who, like him,
sought to bring peace.
He did not turn away from suffering and need.

There is no uncleanliness in his heart. He is pure
though his corporeal body may be soiled;
he has been brutally deprived of its control.

The adversary, a massive brain hemorrhage, stretched forth
his hand upon his brain,
scalpels entered his Sanctuary. Why have You commanded
such destruction of a son of Zion?

All his people are sighing as they search for cures;
they'd give away their treasures, their food to
revive his inert body. See O Lord, how worthless
and powerless you've become to fix this?

All of you who pass along the road of life,
let it not happen to you! Guard your health to avoid
pain like his pain, a blow like the one which has been dealt
unto him by fierce and angry fates.

From above they have hurled fire into his bones,
his muscles, his nerves and broke them.
They've pushed him on his back, made him desolate,
exhausted and spent every hour, every day.

For these things I weep, my eye, yea, my eye sheds tears
for a comforter to restore my soul,
for my child not to be so desolate;
for the enemy-stroke not to prevail.

Did the yoke of my maternal transgressions mark him?
His life has become interwoven with mine. I feed him,
I move his inert limbs, but each time I try to soothe him,
he causes me to strengthen, not to fail.
His courage delivers me into the hands of hope.

I spread out my hands for help,
but there are none to truly comfort him.
The aides around him mean well but they
do not understand the mysteries of the brain,
or the depth of his sorrow. They attend to his body;
but his mind, heart and soul are left to starve.

The Lord is not righteous.
I have rebelled against His empty words.
Hear, all you peoples and behold his pain;
my young son and his maidens have gone into captivity.

Behold, O Lord, for I am in distress, my innards burn,
my heart is turned within me for I have lost hope, rebelled
against the fates yet they laugh their hyena laughter.
His life is like death.

The Weeping Prophet

After forty-seven years it's hard to say
if we named him after my favorite
prophet Jeremiah, or just because
I didn't want our son to blend with
all those Michaels, Kevins and Scotts.

Yirmeyahu was the figure of doom
whose dark passion excited my
young imagination, resonated
the way he revealed his innermost
angst. He was the model of a
genuine being, visionary, foretold
the destruction of the temple just as
our son foretold the financial collapse.
Prophecies fulfilled.

Not so fast! I should have had
more sense, more deep insight.
I should have known he was the
weeping prophet, subjected to pain
and suffering. A prophet whose
writings were excised by the King
who feared him, just as the fates
would obliterate those parts of
our son's brilliant mind that could,
see into the future, dream big,
think different.

He would not bow to greed, nor
demean anyone. Lived and studied
Ghandi's teachings in India, spoke of
peace with Pope John Paul at the Vatican,
learned about war in China, Vietnam, Germany.
Said knowledge was the only route
to seek the truth, to do good. Now he sits
still as a boulder; his temple ruined,
the bleak prophecy realized.

Maybe if he had known that
Jeremiah was not to marry or to
have children, maybe then he would
have stayed in heaven's good graces.
But he didn't know. I failed
to warn him. Maybe if I hadn't
named him after the prophet of doom,
he might have been saved.

A prophesy?

On November 12th, 2014 a bomb hurled by fate exploded in our lives. Should not have tangled with a prophet. How else can one account for a vibrant, 46-year old son, being felled like a mighty sequoia?

Did it bother the fates a doting father stayed home to attend a parent-teacher conference? Or perhaps it was their clever intent to save him? The nine and eleven year-old girls had no idea hell would open when they investigated.

They knocked then banged on the bathroom door shouting in their thin little girl voices, "Daddy, daddy come out!" But all they heard was water running, running, running... an unrelenting deluge that soaked their childhood.

By the time I got to the emergency room he was barely alive. A stroke nurse took me aside, trying to console me. "Fewer than 50% of victims of this type of brain hemorrhage survive," she volunteered. "But, your son was lucky, nearly 20% never make it to the ER." A new view of luck I had never considered.

I stood like an iceberg paralyzed with fear. Where would I find support? From the devastated wife? Terrified little girls? My husband lay at home, just a few weeks past a total knee replacement, unable to walk; deadly bacteria already lurking in his knee.

Our only daughter lived a continent away. She got on the next flight to the US. Eleven weeks later, as our son still teetered in a coma between life and death, his father suffered a stroke. Life as we knew it would *never* be the same. My two loves broken.

We raised our son with the fondest hopes, never contemplated his life would be so altered by a cruel single event. We were about to enter our golden period, but trickster gods turned them into pyrite years.

Perhaps if I had ever contemplated such a terrifying possibility, I would not have been so shattered by the suddenness of it. Would I recommend parents entertain such gruesome eventualities? I don't know.

There is nothing for me to do now but pour out my heart, lament like Yirmeyahu.

Seeds of Destruction

MEDITATION I

A languid July afternoon.
I lie in my hammock
following the dragon cloud
as it shape shifts.
A yellow leaf floats to the ground
whirling in the breeze, resisting
its death.

It's too early for fall, I say.

She brushes her raven hair,
one hundred strokes,
examines her face in the mirror
when she spots the invader.
A silver hair, a snake winding
its way to her neck. She
 pulls it out in one nimble twist.

I am too young for this, she says.

He jumps into the cab aggravated
it's late; his girls will be asleep
by the time he gets home,
too late for a bedtime story.
His head pounds; he rubs his temple,
pops a pill.

I am too young for this, he says.

My Tisha B'av

My Tisha B'av came late
in 2014. Three months and
ten days late in fact, but it
came nevertheless, unbidden,
unexpected as all tragedies are.

Maybe if had known to fast
for 25 hours beforehand,
maybe if I had asked him
about his dreams and why
did he have such a nasty
headache, maybe if I hadn't
bathed and rubbed the
scented cream into my
aging skin, maybe if I had
gone barefoot.

Maybe if I had recited the
kinnot, but how
could I have? I hadn't
written them yet. I was still
a virgin in the realm of
sorrow, naïve of real pain.

Prescience

They glide in the rowboat
down the East River,
he and his two-red headed
girls. The little heads
tuning this way and that
to see Carl Schurz park.
See, see the Crape Myrtle
flowers he asks pointing
up, way up. And though
they can't spot them
they hear the yelps in the
dog run above, imagine
all the puppies wagging
their tails.

Suddenly the
current begins to churn,
run swifter, the waters
now darker, turbulent
as if a storm were coming
yet it's still sunny, the
dark clouds invisible.
He hangs on to the girls
tightly as the boat twists
and turns, rushes wildly
forward. Flows into
an abyss.

Wakes up from the
harrowing dream
sweaty, frightened.
Will you take care
of the girls if something
happens to me? She looks
at him puzzled. It's just
a dream. Go back to sleep.

Forewarning

Maybe that dream was meant
to be his crystal ball,
a soothsayer wizened and
experienced in prognosticating
doom, but he didn't quite read
it that way, brushed it off
like lint off the pinstriped
suit he'd wear to the meeting
that last day when he'd have
much to say, much to do.

He walked between buildings
with his girls, playing a kind
of hide and seek game. He
didn't like the dark maroon
brick walls. Maybe they
reminded him of dried blood.

He wanted to get out of there
but the walls began to inch
closer to one another, created
a narrow tunnel that frightened
the girls and they ran as the
walls were closing in.

He raced all out of breath and
terrified, calling out their pet
names, Squealy! Captain cuddles!
but they were nowhere to be seen.

Meditations on a November Emergency

So the cab driver says, yeah the traffic will get much thicker soon through midtown. You know with the holidays coming and all and all I can see is the beach and the lifeguard station in Surfside and I want to know if it has hoisted the red flag of emergency: stay away, danger, danger the currents will swallow you if you are not a Michael Phelps or Mark Spitz and you are not, you are not though you are a fine, handsome swimmer that women swoon over can't wait to get their paws on your beautiful flesh.

And neither do I want to see the yellow flag that demands extreme caution, something you never exercised, like the time we told you to stay away from motorcycles and you didn't. Came home sheepishly with your arm in a sling and said it was the black ice somewhere on campus.

Getting stopped by the cops at thirteen all because they wanted you on the PAL basketball team. Where did your tall genes come from anyway? Did they come with a secret grenade in your skull? We were so stupid to trust you and yet we did, we do, you fruit of our loins, causing pain even when you don't mean it.

Don't mean it at all what with your peacenik heart and travels to the ashram and going on and on about the magical properties of Chinese traditional medicine. May it work now. Please, please may it. But there isn't traditional medicine except in Chinatown amid the tourists, thirty-dollar Coach bags and soup dumplings and secretly sold rhino horn. Chinese opera with all that exaggerated color with blood red masks meaning bravery. No not found on the Upper East Side, not here where myriad machines buzz and emit rays cooked up by mad scientists spit out electroencephalograms, myelograms, magnetic resonance images and where rich ladies lunch at Via Quadronno.

Oh, crap I almost forgot about the blue and purple flags that say sharks and jellyfish and nasty things that could make me vomit. I feel the sting of a thousand barbs in my skin now and the honking, the honking makes me want to scream but I have to apply shaving cream, or vinegar or piss to my wounds and can't stop and anyway nothing, nothing could issue from my throat. Are we close to 77[th1] Street yet I ask and all I hear back is his blabber in Arabic or Urdu or Punjabi.

1   77th Street & Lexington Ave. on Manhattan's Upper East Side is the location of Lenox Hill Hospital's Emergency Room

Erythra Thalassa

One Israelite crossing
on a life and death journey
a sea of crimson, bubbling,
rushing through the great rifts
between the hemispheres
flooding the sulci and gyri.

In the myriad gray folds
no neuron, no synapse,
no astrocyte,
no oligodendrocyte,
no microglia left dry.
Epic flood.

Then all is silenced.
No cheering on the other shore.
How long the deafening
stillness? How long the ears
shuttered closed?
How long will eyelids
veil his light?

Give it to me straight

So doc, will he ever
wake up? Give it to
me straight.

If consciousness is lost
and the coma develops
minutes or hours after
the head injury, the cause
is likely due to intra-cerebral
bleeding and compression
of the brainstem as
the cerebrum is squeezed
into the foramen magnum
thus injuring the brainstem
which mediates not only
consciousness via the
reticular formation but
vital functions such as
heart rate, breathing, and so on.

Ha?? So will he wake up?
I...I ...want to know.

Let us do a lumbar puncture
some CTs MRIs and EEGs
take a CBC and then I may
possibly shed more light
on your question.

Light? Will he see the
light of day? So you are
giving him a chance
aren't you?
Bless you, doc.

1-800-Please-Help

There weren't any virgins.
Not 72, not even one, but
I clearly saw them:
angelic telephone operators
at an old-fashioned switchboard,
sitting in neat rows
far enough from one another
so their wings didn't tangle.

Through the buzz and celestial
interference they strained to hear
the earthly pleas, but maybe,
maybe, I thought, they'd hear mine.

'Just let him open his eyes'
At first I whispered shyly,
didn't want to overwhelm
them with my greed.
Didn't want to say plain and
simple: I want him back
whole, the way he was,
seeing as they already granted
him life. Then I got bolder,
more urgent.

I shouted, then screamed
but they still refused to hear.
Just kept fussing with all those
cords, keys and jacks,
as if they really meant
to be helpful.

Half Empty or Half Full?

Is the glass half empty,
or half full? Hard to say.
You lie in a coma for weeks
hovering on the edge of life.
Loved ones whisper
in hushed tones around
your bedside,
'wake up daddy'
'you'll get through this, son'

Machines hum a dirge,
tubes enter and exit the
body at odd angles,
make you look like
a space explorer
and indeed, you may be
at this very moment
walking on Uranus
which was once Herschel,
sounded like a *lantsman,*
so you said: why not?

And I know you picked
it because its blue hue
reminded you of *Zeyda's*
eyes and because you
fell in love with its moons,
all Shakespeare's women:
Cordelia and Ophelia and
Bianca, and let's not
forget Desdemona.

But I digress. The stifled
sobs don't wake you,
don't intrude on your
planetary journey.
Will he know us when
he wakes up? She asks,
because she's terrified
to ask *if.*

But if he knows us
and can't move
will it be a victory,
or a failure? And what
if it's the other
way around?

I'd love to know

You sit there like a
beautiful statue, your face
carved in marble, eyes
turned skyward, silent
as a tomb.

I watch you
for signs of movement
I'll take anything, a twitch
of a finger, a tensing of
a cheek muscle, but no,
such feats are still
somewhere in the distant
ocean whose turbulent surf
you'll tame one day, near the
rushing mountain streams
teeming with lavender asters and
golden bush you'll weave
into wreaths for your ladies.

They are there
I know, I have faith
but not the kind
that is blind, that
drops you to your
knees and beseeches
a nonexistent deity.

My faith is in the magic,
the mystery of the
human brain, its
neuroplasticity that
is still in the twenty-
first century as uncharted
as the Greenland ice sheet,
Amazon tribes hidden
in the depths of the jungle,
the Namibian desert,
the geysers of Kamchatka.

But one day we will know
and I'll be ready to
take your outstretched
hand and listen to
the story of your
long journey and how you
fought dehydration and acute
mountain sickness and chilblains
and snow blindness
and how you ascended to the peak.

On Health Insurance

Oh how they loved you
When you were hale and hearty
A winner in his field, earner,
Payer of insurance bills

Then a rupture in the soulless
Love affair, no checks in the mail,
No payment online, no love!
But it must be an error, he's insured.

Did you study the fine print?
Surely not.
We don't cover this, or that,
Or the other, either.

But it's a catastrophic event!
Cries go out to the hapless clerks,
Then to the supervisors, then
To the appeals committees.

But they've all gone deaf and blind,
Their brains in power saver mode.
Power saver equals money saver
Equals promotion, equals atta boy.

If you had read the fine print
You'd have known that
The insurance payment insures
The company, not you, you fool.

Silent Repose

Head cocked in contemplation
on the madness of random events.
Crown of thorns, rays of EEG wires,
eyelids lowered just enough
to cover the shame of putting
others through suffering.

Beard growing, some part of him
alive, flourishes unbowed.
The face serene,
a Jesus after the cross.
Me, a Madonna looking skyward
beseeching, knowing no answer
will issue from a mute swan heaven.

Mother's Day Roses

We sat in utter despair, waiting.
Two women who loved him,
a mother and wife broken
by his brain hemorrhage.

Echoes bounced off the polished
hallway; gurneys passed;
he wasn't on them.
He was a moth in the ICU
hovering too close to flame.

Each of us grieved in our own way;
she a monsoon in India;
I, a windswept, parched Atacama.
A surreal vision appeared,
his neurosurgeon, the God of neuro ICU
handed each of us a bouquet of roses.

Deep as Lake Baikal

His eyes deep as Lake Baikal,
My sorrow deeper yet.

Their incomparable blueness
Of the sky over Rio de Janeiro
How much more intense than
All the lagoons of Turkey's
Turquoise Coast,
More pristine than China's
Five Flower lake.

They ask me to help him,
Free him from bondage
From his contorted body
From his suffering
From the million daily
Indignities he suffers.
Each humiliation a brown leaf
settling on exhausted soil
until the earth is covered
by rotting leaves, buried
under a blanket of frozen,
dirty snow.

I think dark thoughts,
hear tormenting sounds,
spades digging into
frozen soil, earth thudding
against pine.

Clouds passing over lakes,
casting shadows on life within,
innocent of knowledge
of the sun's return,
unaware of fate,
dumb to its meanness.

You Can Say Consistency is the Hobgoblin of Small Minds and Maybe my Mind *is* Small Because I am Frightfully Consistent in Matters of Life and Death

In my clunky atheist way
I pray each day,
each day I pray.

Damn you! Fickle finger of fate,
you deceitful whore.
I beseech you, unveil your
face. No rouge, no mascara
Just give me one true smile.

Just this one time keep your
red tipped claws out of his
flesh. I promise
I won't ask for more.

I'll pay you with gold, wash
your feet with my tears.
Daily I say out loud:
only idiots pray.

Which god is great?
Which god is good?
What has he done for
humanity lately?

Has cancer been cured?
Has ISIS stopped
beheading Infidels,
raping little girls?

The fools blind to the
pathetic failure of prayers.
Can't they see it's all
a matter of chance?

An oak in a storm crushes
An SUV, mother and baby too.
A plane plummets into the
depths, pieces of fuselage
float aimlessly on the calm sea.

And yet I pray,
to my savior, Science
For a stem cell miracle.
I pray each day,
each day I pray.

A Mountain Stream at Moose Creek

The searing pain, red hot,
flesh piercing, tendon
tearing, mind numbing.

Does it purify the spirit?

The dizzying explosions
of neurons firing haywire,
sending signals with no address.

Myriad daily indignities
of the flesh, pea soup
dripping off the chin.

Do they purify the spirit?

Must be so. The fates
wouldn't be so perverse,
so wicked. Isn't it enough
they've opened blood
vessels, Pandora's boxes
filled with mischief?
Spilled their contents,
invited scalpels to join
the raucous orgy, slice
bone like butter, taunted
drills to pierce it?

When all is said and done,
his spirit will be purer
than a mountain stream
at Moose Creek,
more wholesome than
a nubile virgin on her
wedding day,
whiter than a bone
baked in the Kalahari sands.

Small and Monstrous

Who knew little indignities
Could be so monstrous?
No one knows until
It happens to them.

Can't scratch your nose
Can't turn in bed
Can't rub your eye
Can't put food in your mouth

Your brain has rendered your
Neck, arms, hands, legs, feet.
useless. You lie still as a boulder,
helpless like a newborn.

Can't go to the toilet
Can't wipe your butt
Can't dry your snot
Can't push a call button.

So go ahead enjoy
That scratch, that turn,
That wipe, that movement
That lets you know
you are "normal."

A Year Later

When things seem to
settle down, brow wiped
deep breath taken
that's when the emergency
is doubled, tripled,
multiplied into
infinity.

Getting used to horror
is an emergency.
Sitting down calmly
to a hot meal, inhaling
the aroma of the dish
while all's not well,
not well at all
and never will be,
that's the time to
tear off the scab,
to remember.

Push away the plate
call 911, scream,
tear out the hair,
wipe off the shame
of complacency
and feel the pain
all over again.

2015

That January was colder
than a rat's ass; records
broken daily. He rode in
the ambulance bundled
in white blankets that
made me think of burial
cloths. But it was progress
of sorts, he would ascend
to Mt. Sinai where there
would be only one
commandment: recover!

February should have
been kinder, but it wasn't.
It was a double whammy,
lightning striking twice.
Like son, like father—
stroke! Then worse yet,
status epilepticus,
was that the message
of those white blankets?
Lost in the mists of a coma.
Will he ever return?

March came in like a lion
with his hungry maw,
took hold of his brain
infused it with fetid airs.

The doctors fought them
with magic potions and
we fought valiant losing
battles with CIGNA and
hospital administrators
colder than the east ridge
of Antarctica.

Oh, blessed April. He spoke!
I love you Momma. Was it
his birthday, or Pesach that
woke him from a four month
slumber? They have never
seen so many balloons in a
hospital room, nor so much
singing, voices raising above
the din of machines, above
the hushed voices of residents,
whispers of intensivists.

Bloody May. Not so fast,
do not count your chickens
before they are ready to fly
to Helen Hayes coops. The
knives, the drills still thirst
for his skull, the breathing
machines want to pump
life into him once more,
hear the music of his lungs,
but parting will come before
the blooms are off the hyacinths.

A June feast fit for a royal,
a whole ounce of pudding
thanks to the Good Samaritan.
Now braces, therapy, therapy
and pain, pain, pain but
the Hudson River makes it
feel like freedom may be
around the corner. His first
real smile seeing the Father's Day
offerings made by his girls,
and their cartwheels on the lawn.

Back to Westchester in July,
an old haunt from childhood,
not Larchmont, but Port Chester
will do as there's nowhere
else to go. Has anyone ever
seen a homeless quadriplegic?
In the US it's a real possibility.
The surgeon's scalpels, blades
and clamps called him in that
blood thirsty wail, now his heart
not the only pump in his frail body.

In August he says: take me
home please, but it's not time
yet. Must adjust the pump
up, up, up, up to defrost those
frozen limbs, Peak Woo must
peek into the throat, assess
the voice, find that paralyzed
vocal cord, but a prize awaits:
visit to see the home. Home!

Last glimpse.
Moving day approaches.

What a fall celebration in
September: Momma's
birthday and Rosh Hashanah
rolled into one with him
at the table at Plaza 400.
Joy! The ambulette ride is
rough but hearing him whisper
happy birthday worth everything.
And a new doc in the august
panoply of experts, O'Dell, may
he move mountains, or just one finger.

His favorite month, October.
He says: I like the burnt
orange leaves and how they
drift to the ground. I love
carving smiling pumpkins
with my girls, picking apples,
riding with them on hay
wagons. Not this year. This
time the girls carve tiny
pumpkins for daddy. Bring
sunflowers so the sun can shine.

November, home at last, in time
for Thanksgiving. Favorite holiday.
Turkey and stuffing and all
the trimmings for dinner, but
pureed please. Family gathers,
savory smells waft from the
new kitchen, just like always...
almost. The wheelchair doesn't
quite fit against the table.
something is definitely askew.
It's the same daddy, but different.

Must get him into the groove
of his former life. December,
a time to celebrate again,
eat the *latkes* from a huge stack
eat the apple sauce too. Watch
the girls light the menorah. Then
the family ritual, picking a
Christmas tree. Watch the stockings
and decorations go up, reminisce
about them. Hope next year
he can hang the lights himself.

My Life, My Guilt

There's something so crass
about my living now,
all those prosaic
needs: morning coffee,
strong, in the tall mug,
hot shower with the
fig soap from Florence
clean Jockey underwear,
answering the umpteenth
sales call,
paying rent bills.

It goes on and on, no matter
his pain and misery.
He suffers indignities:
aides clean his behind,
his young daughter
feeds the dad who can't
move a muscle by himself,
his sister wipes the dribble
of applesauce from his chin.

But I go off to make dinner
buy green beans and milk,
stop by the cleaners,
pick up the mail,
then plop insensate
in front of the boob tube
watching the regurgitated
news that even an idiot
could recite by heart.

When a Squeeze is Not Just a Squeeze

His girls' toys
clutter the living
room floor.
Book bags, scooters,
packed camp bags
lean against the
wall festooned
with child drawings.

The room is dark.
Window shades
blot out the sun
though a few
rays sneak in.
Photophobia.

The room is stifling.
He can't bear the
air conditioned air
hitting his skin.
Allodynia.

Mom, the stroke
scrambled my brain,
I am sorry.
He whispers so low
I have to bring my
ear to his cracked lips,
but I am happy.

Fifteen months ago
a breathing tube
clogged his throat.
Wires protruded
from his head,
a Jesus with eyes
fixed on me in
silent prayer,
beseeching.

Please, let me play
you the NPR news,
I say, so you ...
...stay connected.
I promise to lower
the volume.
Mom, my hearing is
better than a bat's,
he says, doesn't smile.

I pull over the desk
chair he can't use now.
Still, insists we place
his wheelchair in front
of his computer.

I sit by him, take his
once strong hand
whose grip could
crush walnuts
at Rosh Hashanah,
now contorted, useless.

I feel a slight squeeze,
fingers curling,
not sure if it's meant for me
or just another spasm.

It's the Little Things

Have I ever thought about
what size bite of burger
I want to put in my mouth?
Do I want a big chunk, or small?

Now I do.

Did I ever think how long
I want to chew it,
savor its flavor in my mouth,
move it around with my tongue?

Now I do.

Did I ever think about the coffee,
or tea, or juice I drink?
Sip them fast, or slow
from the cup, or a straw?

Now I do.

Did I ever think
I couldn't turn, scratch,
wash, blow my nose,
clean my ears, cut my nails?

Now I do.

I Scream Into the Void Because it Has Been Obvious Forever There's Nothing Up or Down or Sideways to Call G With a Capital or Even With a Minuscule g

I've always loved best his
photos with the newborn daughters,
peach fuzz headed bundles
still wet from the amniotic sea.

So vulnerable both child and father
as if at any instant either could
disappear, the seeds of trouble
still silently nursing at the
bittersweet tit of the future.

Thousands of images in my albums,
envelopes filled with old scenes
birthdays, vacations, Thanksgivings
fading Polaroids, Kodak prints
and developed film stuck
together like lizard scales
all captured memories
like fireflies in a bottle
by voracious documentarians
keeping the moments forever fresh
like dehydrated milk
without expiration date.

I never cared so much about them.
Now they are my lifeline
I hold on to them as a drowning
woman grasps flotsam

Of them all, these first, miraculous
points of time I like best, for
they hold no hint, no telltale sign
that one of this tender scene
would never be whole again.

Now I keep them stuck in the
frame of the bedroom mirror
so I can remember what
happiness feels like
whenever I want to scream.

Don't!

Chicken in the oven,
dust on the armoire,
unpaid bills piling up,
laundry tumbling in
the dryer until it turns to dust.

Don't fool yourself,
don't delude yourself that
things will never be the same.
You'll still brush your teeth,
reach for the soap bar
in the shower, rummage
for fresh underwear,
turn on the news.

Even in time your
hunger will return.
You'll yearn for a hot meal,
not the bagel you used to
grab on the run, or the
stale donut eaten at midnight,
the last one from DD
before they closed.

You will answer the phone
at last, I'm OK you'll say,
for how can you keep saying
things are bleak. You'll
feel you must lift the callers'
spirit to keep them from
drowning in your sorrow,
and soon you'll start
believing it, almost.

That will be the exact time
to rip open the scab
to remember things
will never be the same.

What is it like?

What is it like to have no hope;
to spend each hour,
each day,
each month,
knowing nothing will change?

The relentless pain
will still have him in its grip.
The inert body will remain mute
to signals from the brain.
The aides will still talk
over his head, their idle
Jamaican chatter as if he
were a mere stone, or a mummy
that needed occasional dusting.

Does his still nimble brain
visit galaxies invisible
to the able bodied? Does he plan
his future in the world-to-come?
No. He wants to plan
for this world.

Mom, can you help me
figure out how to run
for City Council?
My eyes open in surprise.
What do you want to accomplish?
I ask.
Accessible schools, movie theatres,
restaurants.
I want to live.

Yes, my son, I lie,
I'll see what can be done.
He is unable to assess
his own capabilities.

I utter a soundless scream
and wish for his strength,
his courage.

The Scarlet G

You may not see it,
but I know it's there.
I carve it daily in the flesh
of my forehead, a raw
scarlet G.

Why? You might ask
and I'd say
take one look, just one
look at what's become
of my child.

He lies still as stone
I move, I come, I go,
I could even dance.
He cannot bring food to his lips;
I eat what I want, when I want.

He depends on the kindness
of strangers
to clean his body, brush his teeth
however rough, perfunctory;
I revel in the luxury of my bath.

He stares at the ceiling and on
lucky days, at the sky;
perhaps a TV screen, a program
of the aide's choice.
I can travel, see the hills, the ocean.

His main visitors are aides,
therapists, doctors,
sometimes government inspectors
to see if he still really needs help.
I visit with friends.

Is it any wonder I carry it with me
everywhere I go?
Its weight pushes me closer,
ever closer
into the earth.

Luck?

Luck is not a four-leaf clover;
it is not a win at the lottery.
Luck is a state of mind.
You decide what luck is.

For me luck used to be
outliving Hitler, surviving
a communist regime
to drink liberty in the USA,
to wake up to an
intact family.

Now my luck is
seeing him eat without
a feeding tube,
hearing him respond
albeit slowly and quietly,
being able to touch his
inert, contorted hand,
to stroke the hair on his
reassembled skull.

He lies reclined
in his wheelchair grievously
stricken; probably
for life,
unable to do anything
for himself.

He looks up at me
with his clear blue eyes
and says softly:
I am the luckiest man
on the Upper East Side
—except for dad.

The Benefits of Self-Deception

Never say never.
It's my mantra. It's how
I greet my morning.
I have learned how to skirt reality,
ignore the hopeless prognosis.

When man first walked on land
did he look at the sky and say,
one day, we shall fly like birds?

Did Anne Miller with a 107° fever
and deadly streptococcal infection
dream in her delirium of penicillin?

Did earthlings toiling on land look
at the harvest moon and say, Neil
Armstrong's footprints will be here?

I want the impossible to become
possible;
I'll grab the infinitesimal chance
with my teeth and won't let go.

Picture, if you will...

MEDITATION 4

Picture, if you will,
your young self, standing
in front of a mirror,
brushing your teeth.
You look, then look again;
who is that old man ?
Bags under the eyes,
ruts in parchment skin.

You turn around.
No one's there,
it's you; suddenly
decades older.
You stand in sheer shock;
no one changes so quickly.

Picture, if you will,
you laying on a beach
perfecting your golden tan.
You look, then look again;
an icy wind churns the waves,
snowflakes thick as marshmallows
settle on your eyelashes.

You look around.
All the bathers gone,
the sky a steel gray sheet.
Your frozen body shivers,
you rise groping for explanation;
nothing changes so quickly.

Picture, if you will,
stepping into a morning shower.
You reach for the soap,
turn on the spray...
When you open your eyes
you lie on a gurney, blood
gushes through your brain,
never to shower again.

Like a Firefly

Dancing specks of light,
one moment here, then there
then here again. I try to see them
as constellations in heaven,
but they don't stay still
enough to discern a pattern.

They dazzle my imagination,
light up the darkness,
ephemeral jewels
making life sweeter,
soon they'll be gone.

Gone like him who first
taught me to see their
fiery dances, who himself
is a jewel making life
bittersweet, who never
stood still enough for me
to discern the pattern of
his life, now stillness is
all he knows, all I know.

Stable

My favorite new word
I roll it on my tongue,
try it on for size.
It fits! It's perfect.

When friends and neighbors
approach me, meaning well
and ask: how is he?
What shall I say?

Should I enumerate
the myriad tribulations,
procedures, medical
disasters, surgeries?

Perhaps I should tell
all about his searing pain,
or the utter hopelessness
of his condition?

He is stable, I say with a smile
on my lips, a stone in
the pit of my stomach.
My mind sees him jumping
off the lifeguard's perch
to save a drowning swimmer.

A Note About Jeremy's Song

Jeremy has always been an avid consumer and lover of music. When the stroke severely restricted his ability to attend concerts and participate in cultural activities, his parents engaged two outstanding musicians—Ken Hatfield, a jazz guitarist, composer and arranger (Kenhatfield.com) and Eric Hoffman a jazz singer and trombonist—to play for Jeremy at home. Jeremy, Ken and Eric developed a bond of friendship over their mutual appreciation of music and its ability to heal.

This song was born in March, on the eve of the 2020 pandemic, when Jeremy expressed a deep desire to coauthor a song with me, dedicated to Diana and their daughters. He proposed some of the lyrics before he fell ill and was hospitalized with COVID-19. Through Jeremy's illness, hospitalization, miraculous survival and recovery, the musicians and I fine-tuned the lyrics. Ken and Eric wrote and recorded the music.

I hope that the inspiration and love that shine through this song, bring joy to anyone who listens to *The Time I Spend with You.*

"The Time I Spend with You"

JEREMY'S SONG

Happiness is a red balloon
Happiness is the sun and moon
Happiness is watching my ladies playing.

Happiness is a soothing tune
Happiness is the sun and moon
Happiness is the time I spend with you.

Life is a rollercoaster,
Often crazy, sometimes broke.
Hold on tight, it's no joke .... my friend.

Life's filled with tears and laughter
Never know just what you'll get
yet each bit, seems to fit.
Life's a precious gift... filled with

Happiness like a day in June
Happiness like the sun and moon
Happiness like each moment spent with you.

Roam the byways of your mind
where your memories reside
Wondrous souvenirs await ... you there...
a-round every corner, you'll find
angels, sages, demons too.

Face to face without fear,
loved ones always near...
like the memories of a day in June, the
radiance of the sun and moon.

Happiness is the time I spend with you.
Happiness is the time I spend with you.

The Time I Spend With You (Jeremy's Song)

Jeremy Berkovits, Annette Berkovits,
Ken Hatfield & Eric Hoffman

Lead-Sheet

THE TIME I SPEND WITH YOU

About the Author

Annette Libeskind Berkovits: scientist, educator, conservationist, and author, was born in Kyrgyzstan and grew up in postwar Poland and the fledgling state of Israel before coming to America at age sixteen.

Culminating her three-decade career with the Wildlife Conservation Society in New York as Senior Vice President and recognized by the National Science Foundation for her outstanding leadership in the field, Annette spearheaded the institution's science education programs throughout the nation and the world.

Despite being uprooted from country to country, Berkovits has channeled her passions into language study and writing. She has published two memoirs, short stories, selected poems, and completed a debut novel. This is her first poetry chapbook. Her stories and poems have appeared in Silk Road Review: a Literary Crossroads; Persimmon Tree; American Gothic: a New Chamber Opera; Blood & Thunder: Musings on the Art of Medicine; and in The Healing Muse.

Her first memoir, In the *Unlikeliest of Places*, a story of her remarkable father's survival, was published by Wilfrid Laurier University Press in September 2014 and reissued in paperback in 2016. Her second memoir, *Confessions of an Accidental Zoo Curator*, was published in April 2017. Her historical novel, *To Swallow the World*, is nearing completion.

Please visit: **annetteberkovits.com** for more information.

Acknowledgments

The following poems in this volume have been previously published:

When a Squeeze is Not Just a Squeeze, published in Blood and Thunder, Musings on the Art of Medicine, The University of Oklahoma, College of Medicine, Fall 2017 volume

Don't!, published in The Healing Muse, A Journal of Literary & Visual Arts; Center for Bioethics and Humanities; SUNY Upstate Medical University, Volume 17 Number 1, Fall 2017

1-800-Please-Help, published in The Healing Muse, A Journal of Literary & Visual Arts; Center for Bioethics and Humanities; SUNY Upstate Medical University, Volume 18 Number 1, Fall 2018

Erythra Thalassa, published in Blood and Thunder, Musings on the Art of medicine, The University of Oklahoma, College of Medicine, Fall 2019 volume

Other works by Annette Libeskind Berkovits

In the Unlikeliest of Places

Nachman Libeskind's remarkable story is an odyssey through crucial events of the twentieth century. With an unshakable will and a few drops of luck, he survives a pre-war Polish prison; witnesses the 1939 Nazi invasion of Lodz and narrowly escapes; is imprisoned in a brutal Soviet gulag where he helps his fellow inmates survive, and upon regaining his freedom treks to the foothills of the Himalayas, where he finds and nearly loses the love of his life. Later, the crushing communist regime and a lingering postwar anti-Semitism in Poland drive Nachman and his young family to Israel, where he faces a new form of discrimination. Then, defiantly, Nachman turns a pocketful of change into a new life in New York City, where a heartbreaking promise leads to his unlikely success as a modernist painter that inspires others to pursue their dreams.

With just a box of tapes, Annette Libeskind Berkovits tells more than her father's story: she builds an uncommon family saga and reimagines a turbulent past. In the process she uncovers a stubborn optimism that flourished in the unlikeliest of places.

"This is a book that works on so many levels: as the biography of a Polish Jew who narrowly escapes two murderous totalitarian systems, as a personal journey that leads to a new life in the United States marked by optimism and accomplishment—and, above all, as the beautiful, heartfelt

tribute of a daughter to her remarkable father."
– *Andrew Nagorski, author of Hitlerland: American Eyewitnesses to the Nazi Rise to Power (2012)*

"The deeper I went into In the Unlikeliest of Places the more I found my eyes tearing up—not from the suffering of victims of the Holocaust but from the beauty of the extraordinary courage and success of Nachman Libeskind. It is, of course, the success of a whole family, a whole people refusing to accept defeat, but it's especially the defiance and joy in his spirit that is so moving. When he goes to Berlin to see the Jewish Museum, designed by his son, Daniel Libeskind, and when he takes up painting in his eighties, not as an old man's busywork but with craft, power, verve, and a brilliant sense of color and composition—those victories moved me more than any recent book on the Holocaust and survival. That man! You're going to love him and love the people who supported and believed in him, especially his wife Dora and his children—Annette and Daniel—and his grandchildren."
– *John J. Clayton, author of Many Seconds into the Future (2014) and Mitzvah Man (2011)*

Published by Wilfrid Laurier University Press in 2014, hardcover edition ISBN: 978-1-77112-066-1; reissued in paperback in 2016, ISBN: 978-1-77112-248-1

Confessions of an Accidental Zoo Curator

From cougars, orangutans, supersize snakes, fugitive pigs, and a shocked New York City cabbie, Confessions is fascinating, and often hilarious. Berkovits masterfully regales readers with stories that give the inside scoop on what went on behind the scenes at one of the world's most famous zoos with facts that read like fiction! Her tales will surprise and enlighten. A must read for all animal lovers and those interested in the future of wildlife.

"...a remarkable story, fascinating and unique...with a deft blend of personal insight and eloquent story-telling, Berkovits takes us from a remote village in Kyrgyzstan to the Bronx Zoo... from neophyte to international leader in her field."
—*William Conway, former President of the Wildlife Conservation Society and Director of the Bronx Zoo*

"...a story that goes far beyond its title. Berkovits goes from a difficult childhood devoid of any real animal connections, to become one of the world's foremost leaders in wildlife conservation education... fascinating and inspiring."
— *Alan Rabinowitz PhD, Zoologist, Author, CEO Panthera*

Published by Tenth Planet press; March 2017,
ISBN: 978-0998757803

Coming Soon

To Swallow the World- a riveting coming-of-age novel set in pre WWII Warsaw, Poland, and Spain during the Spanish Civil War as well as pre and post war France. A rebellious young woman caught up in personal tragedy and swept up by historical events struggles to understand the difference between ideals and reality; between love and infatuation.

For more information visit: **annetteberkovits.com**

Made in the USA
Monee, IL
14 November 2020